In the Days of the Dinosaurs

The Nesting Place

Story by Beverley Randell

Illustrations by Ben Spiby

Long, long ago,
in the springtime,
a big herd
of Maiasaura
was on the move.

More and more Maiasaura
walked out of the forest
and down to the nesting place.

There were a great many
old nests beside the lake.
The nesting place was enormous.

Many of last year's nests were broken.

The Maiasaura took mud
from the old nests
to make new ones.

Long-head, a young mother,
worked hard.
When she had a big pile of mud,
she scooped it out
and lined it with leaves.

Now that her nest was ready,
Long-head could lay her eggs.
Around she went,
around and around the nest,
until she had laid 20 eggs.
Then she put some leaves and some sand
on top of them.

The sun and the leaves
would keep the eggs warm
until the babies were ready to hatch.

At last, weeks later,
Long-head could hear little cries.
Some of the eggs were broken.
Some of the babies
were starting to push their way
out into the sunshine.

The babies were too small to walk around.
They were too small to find things to eat.
Long-head had to hurry away
to get food for them.

But when Long-head left her babies,
a fast little meat-eating dinosaur
saw her go.

It ran between the nests
and past all the other Maiasaura.
Then it darted over to Long-head's nest.

11

When Long-head
came back,
she chased
the meat-eater away.

Two of her babies
had gone, but
Long-head still had
lots of babies
to feed.

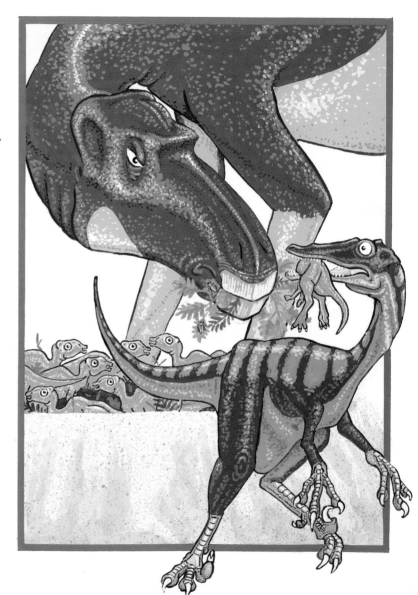

She fed them
with little ferns
and sweet
green leaves.
Some of the leaves
had little beetles
on them.
The babies
liked to eat
leaves and insects.

Weeks went by,
and the babies grew bigger.
Every day, their legs grew stronger.

It was time for the herd to move on.

Long-head was lucky.
She had **eight** young ones left,
but some of the other mothers
on the outside of the nesting place
had only two or three.

All the Maiasaura and their young ones
went off together to feed in the forest.

The enormous nesting place
would be empty again,
until next year....